Pegasus Active Reading

WORLD'S GREAT INVENTORS

Compiled and Edited by
Manpreet K. Aden

CONTENT

1. Introduction 4

2. Alexander Graham Bell 7

3. Albert Einstein 22

4. Alexander Fleming 39

5. Thomas Alva Edison 49

6. The Wright Brothers 64

7. Charles Babbage 77

8. Rudolf Diesel 88

9. James Watt 96

10. Louis Braille 111

INTRODUCTION

Imagine a world without a telephone, computer, an airplane and most importantly electricity. But the world was such long back until there came a few remarkable people, called inventors, who changed the world for the better. The world was altered by these 'inventors' because human beings have always wanted and have looked for change.

An idea is all it takes to make an invention but it is years and years of hard work that brings forth a workable version of that idea. Inventors have an unending zeal to face challenges, solve problems, to find and explore new ways to do things and to make a brighter future. These talented people have left a significant mark on the world and their inventions are still put to use decades after they are gone. With gradual effort and using their skills they have changed the shape of metals, and have manipulated and created objects so that life becomes easier and safer for everyone.

Including the **Greatest Inventors** in our greatest series has a purpose. This series makes the young minds familiar with those remarkable men who are responsible for changing the world, making it a better world. These young minds that yearn to explore more would learn from their example. In turn, they would realise that sky is just the beginning and that imagination and innovation have no set boundaries.

Alexander Graham Bell

Alexander Graham Bell was a Scottish born American inventor and a scientist. The invention of telephone was among his greatest inventions including many others. He mostly received his education through numerous experiments in sound and by helping and learning from his father's work on Visible Speech for the deaf.

Early Years

Alexander Graham Bell was born Alexander Bell on March 3, 1847, in Edinburgh, Scotland. He was the second son of Alexander Melville Bell and Eliza Grace Symonds Bell. He had two brothers: Melville James Bell (1845-70) and Edward Charles Bell (1848-67). Both his brothers died of tuberculosis.

Bell's mother

When, Alexander was 10 years old he urged his father to give him a middle name just like his two brothers. So, on his 11th birthday, his father allowed him to use 'Graham' as his middle name. However, to his family and friends, he remained 'Aleck'.

As a youth, Alexander Graham Bell showed a curious nature regarding the world around him. While still young, he could mimic voices. His grandfather Alexander Bell was a well-known professor and

Mimic to copy someone's voice, behaviour or movements to make others laugh

teacher of elocution and had a great influence over young bell. His mother too encouraged him in his experiments and taught him piano despite her increasing deafness, which started when Alexander was 12 years old. This taught Alexander to look past people's disadvantages and to find solutions to help them.

Alexander Graham Bell was homeschooled by his mother. He received one year of formal education in a private school and spent two years at Edinburgh's Royal High School. Though a mediocre student, he displayed an uncanny interest in sciences, especially biology while disregarding the other subjects. He also displayed an uncommon ability to solve problems. When he was 12 years of age, he used to play with a friend in a grain mill owned by his friend's father. There he learnt the process of dehusking wheat. Alexander, when he returned home, built a device with rotating paddles with sets of nail brushes that easily dehusked the wheat. This was his first invention.

After completing his studies at school, he went to London to live with his grandfather, Alexander

Elocution it is the ability to speak and read aloud publically in a clear, correct manner
Mediocre it is something ordinary
Uncanny it is something difficult to explain; not normal

Bell who taught elocution. During his stay with his grandfather, Alexander learnt to speak clearly and with conviction.

Early Attempts to Follow his Passion

Meanwhile, Alexander's elder brother, Melville, had followed in his father's footsteps and had become an authority on elocution and speech correction. Though young Alexander too was trained to carry forward the family business but he had other ideas.

At 16, Alexander Graham Bell accepted a position of pupil teacher at Weston House Academy in Elgin, Scotland. Here he taught elocution and music to students. The next few years, he attended the University of Edinburgh where he joined his brother Melville. At the end of the term, Alexander returned home and joined his father in promoting Melville Bell's technique of Visible Speech. This technique taught the deaf to align specific phonetic symbols with a particular position of the speech organs. By now Alexander had developed a great interest in the transmission of sound.

Technique the manner of doing something which also requires some skill
Phonetic it concerns symbols that represent the different speech sounds
Transmission a process where something is passed from one to another

Between 1865 and 1870, a lot of change took place in the Bell household. In 1867, the family moved to London and Alexander returned to teaching in Western House Academy. During his stay, he started to experiment with electricity to convey sound. It was also during this year that Alexander's younger brother, Edward, died of tuberculosis. The following year, he once again became his father's apprentice. During this time, his health suffered though he managed to recover. Then, he started staying with his family and soon took full charge of his father's London operations while Melville lectured in America. By now, Melville had married and started a family. He had even started his own elocution school and was successful. However, suddenly in 1870, the family went into a crisis with the death of Melville due to complications from tuberculosis.

It was then that Alexander's father decided to move the family to Newfoundland. On an earlier trip, he had seen that the environment there had cured him of his illness. In the beginning, though Alexander was ill, he wanted to stay in London and establish himself. But when he realized that

Apprentice *a person who works for someone for a fixed time to learn a trade*

his own health was in jeopardy, he agreed to move. So, after settling all their affairs, in July 1870, the family settled in Brantford, Ontario, Canada. There, Alexander's health improved, and he set up a workshop to continue his study of the human voice. He called his workshop, his 'dreaming place' and continued with his experiments working with electricity and sound.

Passion for Shaping the Future

In 1871, Melville Bell, Sr. was invited to teach at the Boston School for Deaf Mutes. However, as working there clashed with his numerous tours, he declined the position to teach there. He, however, recommended Alexander in his place. The younger Bell quickly accepted the position. Combining his father's system of Visible Speech and some of his own methods, he achieved remarkable success. It was during his tours that he continued his experiments with his 'harmonic telegraph'. The idea behind his device was that messages could be sent using a single wire if the messages were sent at different pitches.

As the school had no funds to hire Bell for another semester, he had to leave working at the school.

Jeopardy a dangerous situation where there is possibility of harm to or loss of something or someone

In 1872, Alexander set out on his own and started tutoring deaf children in Boston. It was during this time that he met two of his students —George Sanders and Mabel Hubbard—meeting whom would set him on a new course.

After one of his tutoring sessions with Mabel, Bell sat talking with her father, Gardiner, about his ideas of how several telegraph transmissions might be sent on the same wire if they were transmitted on different harmonic frequencies. Hubbard was interested in Bell at once. It was because he too was trying to find a way to improve telegraph transmissions, which then carried only one message at a time. Hubbard then was able to convince Thomas Sanders, father of George Sanders who was Bell's student, to support the idea by financing it.

Gardiner Hubbard

Between 1873 and 1874, Alexander Graham Bell spent long days and nights trying to perfect the harmonic telegraph. But then he was sidetracked with another idea of transmitting human voice over wires. The diversion frustrated Gardiner Hubbard. It was because he knew that another inventor, Elisha Gray, was working on a multiple-signal telegraph. Several others had also been working along the same lines. In an attempt to make Bell refocus on his efforts, Hubbard hired Thomas Watson, who was a skilled electrician. Watson immediately understood how to develop the tools and instruments Bell needed to continue his project. But Watson soon took interest in Bell's idea of voice transmission. The two men liked and understood each other perfectly from the beginning. It was an excellent partnership with Bell as the ideas man and Watson who had the expertise to put Bell's ideas into reality.

Through 1874 and 1875, Bell and Watson laboured on both the harmonic telegraph and a voice transmitting device. Hubbard insisted that they should give priority to the harmonic telegraph. But soon, he discovered that the two

Diversion *to change the course of someone or something; something which breaks someone's attention while something else was happening*

men had conceptualized the mechanism for voice transmission. Without wasting any time, Hubbard filed for a patent. Though the idea was protected for the time being but the device for transmitting sound was yet to be made.

But then suddenly things changed for the better. Bell and Watson started experimenting with acoustic telegraphy. Then, on June 2, 1875, Watson accidentally plucked one of the reeds and Bell, who was at the receiving end of the wire, heard the overtones of the reed. Overtones were essential for transmitting speech. It then became clear to Bell that only one reed was required to create sound instead of multiple reeds. This led to the invention of "gallows" sound-powered telephone. This telephone could send indistinct, voice-like sounds to the other end but not clear speech. Immediately, Bell filed for a patent. It was three days later, after he had filed the patent, that he tasted success.

Inspired to experiment further, Bell and Watson worked harder. Then, something happened on March 10, 1867, that changed the future. That day, Bell and Watson were as usual experimenting

Patent *it is the right given to an inventor to manufacture, sell or use his invention for a period of time*
Acoustic *it is related to the manner in which sound is heard*
Mechanism *are the moving parts of a machine that do a task; it is also the method of doing something*

in their laboratory. Bell was bent over the liquid transmitted, suddenly he shouted, "Mr. Watson, come here. I want to see you!" It is clear that Bell heard a noise over the wire and called his assistant who was in the adjacent room. In any case, Watson heard Bell's voice through the wire and thus received the first telephone call.

Bell continued his experiments and then brought home the first working model of his telephone. To further promote the idea of the telephone, Bell conducted a series of public demonstrations, ever increasing the distance between the two telephones. At the Centennial Exhibition in Philadelphia, in 1876, Bell demonstrated the working of the telephone to the Emperor of Brazil, Dom Pedro II, who exclaimed, "My God, it talks!" The invention of telephone now occupied the front page of every newspaper.

First working model of telephone

Several other demonstrations followed, each at a greater distance than the last.

Bell and his partners, Hubbard and Sanders tried to sell the patent outright to Western Union but the company refused saying that it was merely a toy. Then, The Bell Telephone Company was created on July 9, 1877.

In the same year on July 11, Alexander Graham Bell married Mabel Hubbard, his former student and the daughter of Gardiner Hubbard, his initial financial backer. Over the course of the next year, Alexander's fame grew and he along with his wife travelled to Europe for demonstrations of his discovery. While there, the Bells' first child, Elsie May, was born. Upon their return to the United States, Bell was summoned

Bell with his wife Mabel and children

to Washington D.C. to defend his telephone patent from lawsuits by others claiming they had invented the telephone or had conceived of the idea before Bell.

Over the next 18 years, the Bell Telephone Company faced over 550 court challenges but the company did not lose any challenge and continued to grow successfully. By 1886, there were more then 150,000 telephones in the United States. By now a lot of improvement had been made in the telephone including adding a microphone. With the addition of the microphone the people did not had to shout to be heard on the other side.

In January 1915, Bell made a transcontinental phone call to Thomas Watson, his associate, from New York City to San Francisco, over a distance of 3, 400 miles.

Making a call

Pursuing his Passion

Despite his success, Alexander Graham Bell was not a businessman. As he became more affluent, he turned over business matters to Hubbard. He, in the mean time, returned to invent more and was inclined towards his intellectual pursuits. In 1880, he was awarded the French Volta Prize for his invention. With the money that he received, he established the Volta Laboratory in Washington, an experimental facility devoted to scientific discovery and further development in the field of sound and communications. During this time he also discovered new techniques to teach speech to the deaf. He even worked with Helen Keller. There he developed a metal jacket to assist patients with lung problems, conceptualized the process for producing methane gas from waste material, developed a metal detector to locate bullets in bodies, and invented an audiometer to test a person's hearing. He continued to work towards helping the deaf and in 1890, established 'the American Association to Promote the Teaching of Speech to the Deaf.'

World's Great Inventors

Among his first inventions after the invention of telephone was the 'photophone'. It was a device which enabled sound to be transmitted on a beam of light. Bell and his assistant, Charles Sumner Tainter, had developed the photophone. Bell regarded the photophone as "the greatest invention I have ever made; greater than the telephone."

Later Life

In 1885, he bought land in Nova Scotia and built a home there. Here too, he continued with his experiments particularly in the field of aviation. Then, in 1888, he co-founded the National Geographic Society.

In the last 3 decades of his life, Bell was involved in a wide range of projects, pursuing them at a furious page. He worked on inventions in flight (the tetrahedral kite), scientific publications (*Science* magazine), and exploration of the earth (*National Geographic* magazine).

Bell died peacefully, with his wife by his side, in Baddeck, Nova Scotia, Canada, on August 2, 1922. The entire telephone system was shut down for

Aviation *is a term associated with the designing, manufacturing and flying of an airplane*

one minute to pay tribute to his life. A few months later, Mabel too passed away. Alexander Graham Bell's contribution to the modern world and his technologies was enormous. He had a rare curiosity to keep searching, striving, to learn and to create.

Albert Einstein

Albert Einstein was born in Ulm, Württemberg, Germany in 1879. He developed the special and general theories of relativity. In 1921, he won the Nobel Prize for physics for explaining the photoelectric effect. He is the most influential physicist of the 20th century. He died on April 18, 1955, in Princeton, New Jersey.

Early Life

Albert Einstein was born on March 14, 1879 in Ulm, Württemberg, Germany, in a secular, middle-class Jewish family. His father, Hermann Einstein, was a salesman and engineer who, later with his brother, founded an electrochemical factory that manufactured electrical equipment in Munich, Germany. The factory had had moderate success for a while. His mother, Pauline Koch, ran the family household. Einstein had a sister Maria, lovingly called Maja. She was born two years after him.

Einstein always said that there were two "wonders" that deeply affected his life. The first wonder happened when he was five years old. It was then that he had first seen a compass. He was completely amazed when he saw invisible forces deflecting the needle. The second wonder happened when Einstein was 12. Then he had first discovered a geometry book. He called the book, my "sacred little geometry book".

Einstein attended elementary school at the Luitpold Gymnasium in Munich, where he excelled in his studies. He also enjoyed music and even praised God, chanting religious songs on the way to school. However, he strongly disliked the Prussian-style education system that stopped any sign of creativity. One teacher even told him that he would never be able to amount to anything.

In 1889, the Einstein family often had a young medical student, Max Talmud, for dinner. He had a great influence on the young Albert. Talmud became an informal tutor to young Albert and introduced him to higher mathematics and philosophy. One of the books Talmud shared with Albert who was 16 was a children's science series by Aaron Bernstein, *Naturwissenschaftliche Volksbucher. In this series, the author imagined that he was riding alongside electricity that was travelling inside a telegraph wire.* Einstein began to wonder what a light beam would look like if you could run alongside it at the same speed? This thought of the relative speed to the stationary observer and the observer moving with the light continued to dominate Einstein's ideas for the next 10 years. If light were a wave, then the light beam should appear stationary, like a frozen wave. Yet,

Relative it means that something is taken into consideration depending on its position and relation to something else

in reality, the light beam is moving. This paradox led him to write his first "scientific paper" at age 16, "The Investigation of the State of Aether in Magnetic Fields."

However, in 1894, Hermann Einstein's company failed to get an important contract to electrify the city of Munich and thus the factory suffered a great loss. He then was forced to move his family to Milan, Italy. In order to prevent any disruption in Albert's studies, he was left at a boarding house in Munich to finish his education at the Luitpold Gymnasium. Alone, miserable, and opposing the prospect that he would have to join and do military duty at 16, Einstein decided to leave school. Albert left the school after he got a note of excuse written by a doctor and travelled to Milan to unite with his parents. His parents were surprised to see him there and then grew troubled

Young Einstein

Paradox *a statement that has two different ideas which can be true*
Contract *it means an official agreement between two people or parties*

when they realized the problems that Albert would face as a school dropout with no employment skills.

Fortunately, Einstein could apply directly to the Eidgenössische Polytechnische Schule (Swiss Federal Polytechnic School) in Zürich, Switzerland. Though he had no high school diploma but he would be eligible for the school if he managed to clear their stiff entrance test. Albert scored excellently in mathematics and physics but scored fairly in chemistry, French and biology. It was because of his exceptional mathematic scores that he was admitted to the polytechnic school. He was however required to complete his formal schooling. He then attended a special high school run by Jost Winteler in Aarau, Switzerland. He graduated from the school in 1896.

During this time, he also gave up on his German Citizenship. He remained stateless until he got the Swiss Citizenship in 1901. Einstein recalls that he had spent some of the happiest years of his life in Zürich . It was also here that he met students who became his loyal friends. Among them were Marcel Grossmann, a mathematician and Besso,

---

Physics *a branch of science that deals with energy, matter, motion and force*
Chemistry *a branch of science that deals with the structure and properties of substances*
Polytechnic *an institution for higher education which mainly offers scientific and technical education*

with whom he discussed at length about time and space. He also met his future wife Mileva Maric at the polytechnic.

Also, Einstein's became lifelong friends with the Winteler family, who had given them boarding. Winteler's daughter became Albert's first love. Einstein's sister, Maja, also later married the Winteler's son Paul.

A Time of Crisis

After graduating from the Polytechnic Institute in 1900, Albert Einstein faced a major crisis of his life. While at the Polytechnic, he was an irregular student as he had already read advanced subjects on his own while old ideas were being taught at the institute. Moreover, Einstein left a bad impression on the teachers of the institute. So, after his graduation, Einstein was unable to find any teacher from the institute who was ready to write him a letter of recommendation so he could take a job. In the end, Heinrich Weber, an institute teacher, did write for him a letter of recommendation due to which he was turned down from many jobs.

Recommendation *it is a letter written to an authority figure saying that someone in particular would be suitable for a specific job as a favour*

Also during this time, Einstein's relationship with Mileva had deepened and he wanted to get married to her. However, his parents were opposed to this marriage because of Mileva's Serbian background as she followed an Eastern Orthodox Christian religion. But Einstein continued to see Mileva and they had a daughter in 1902 though it remains unknown whether she died or was given for adoption.

This was the lowest point in Einstein's life. He was unable to find a job and therefore he could not marry Mileva. Also, his father's business had once again turned out as a failure. Desperate, Einstein started taking tuitions but he could not keep these jobs for long. It was then in 1902 that his friend Marcel Grossmann's father came to his rescue. He recommended him for a position as a clerk in the Swiss patent office in Bern, Switzerland. About this time, Einstein's father

Einstein with wife Mileva

Orthodox *something which is accepted in society like a philosophy or a doctrine*

became seriously ill and gave Einstein blessings to marry Mileva shortly before he died. Now that he had a steady income, Einstein was able to marry Mileva on January 6, 1903. In May, 1904 their first son Hans Albert was born while their second son Eduard was born in 1910.

A Change on the Horizon

Einstein's work at the patent office came as a blessing to him. While working at the patent office, Einstein needed to analyze the patent applications, a task which he easily and quickly managed. Once he had completed his work, Einstein had time to ponder on the thought, what would happen if one raced alongside a light beam?

While at the polytechnic, Einstein had studied Scottish physicist James Maxwell's electromagnetic theories which described the nature of light. While studying the theories, Einstein had discovered a fact which was unknown to Maxwell. He discovered that the speed of light remained constant. But this fact violated Isaac Newton's laws of motion because according to Newton's theory there is no absolute

---

Electromagnetic *a substance having both magnetic and electric fields*
Theory *it is a set of ideas that explain why certain things happen or exist*

velocity. This insight helped Einstein to formulate his **Theory of Relativity**.

Then, in 1905, Einstein submitted his paper for his doctorate and had four papers published in *Annalen der Physik*, a renowned physics journal. The year 1905 was the "miracle year" for Einstein. His four papers were on—the photoelectric effect, Brownian motion, special relativity, and the equivalence of matter and energy. These papers changed the ideas held by modern physics and brought him into the spotlight of the world.

In his paper on photoelectric effect, Einstein applied the Quantum Theory to explain the photoelectric effect. In his paper on matter and energy, Einstein deduced the well-known equation $E=mc^2$, suggesting that tiny particles of matter could be converted into huge amounts of energy. This also explained the energy source of the sun and stars. This theory was later used in the development of nuclear power.

There have been claims saying that Einstein's wife Mileva had helped him write these papers. But

---

Quantum Theory *according to this theory energy exists in undivided units*
Energy *it is the source of power; it is the ability to do something*
Nuclear *connected or related to atomic energy*

so far no actual proof has been given to establish the claims. Einstein, however, credits that his conversations with Michele Besso helped him develop his theory of relativity.

Einstein's papers, however, were not given much importance by the physics community in 1905. It was not until the papers were read by Max Planck, the most influential physicist of the time and founder of Quantum Theory, that the papers were given a second chance. Planck greatly praised Einstein and even confirmed his theory. Einstein was then invited to lecture at international meetings. Quickly Einstein rose in the academic world. With his new fame, a number of job offers also came to Einstein. He was offered a series of positions at increasingly prestigious institutions, including the University of Zürich, the University of Prague, the Swiss Federal Institute of Technology, and also at the University of Berlin. It was here that Einstein served as the director of the Kaiser Wilhelm Institute for Physics from 1913 to 1933.

While his fame spread to all corners of the world, Einstein's marriage started to fall apart.

His constant travel and intense study of his work, the arguments which concerned their children and their finances led Einstein to conclude that his marriage would not work. It was during this time that Einstein started an affair with his cousin, Elsa Löwenthal. Einstein married her after he had given divorce to Mileva in 1919.

Einstein with second wife Elsa

Einstein's Theory of Relativity

Between 1907 and 1915, Einstein developed his general theory of relativity. He considered his earlier theory to be flawed as the theory had no mention of gravitation or acceleration. He considered his general theory of relativity to be a masterpiece. He was convinced that this theory was absolutely correct.

Flaw a defect; it means that something does not work properly
Acceleration the rate at which something or someone increases its speed

His general theory of relativity also predicted that a measurable deflection of light would take place around the sun when a planet or another sun would pass next to it. In 1919, his predictions were confirmed in the observations of British astronomer Sir Arthur Eddington during the solar eclipse of 1919. The picture clearly showed the light from a star slightly bent or curved by the gravitational force of the sun. Einstein's theory was proved and he became an acclaimed physicist overnight. Then in 1921, Albert Einstein received word that he had been awarded the Nobel Prize for Physics. However, he received his Noble Prize for the explanation of the photoelectric effect rather than for the theory of relativity.

Solar eclipse of 1919

In the 1920s, Einstein continuing with his new discoveries brought forth the science of cosmology.

Deflection *it is the sudden change in the direction of something which is moving*

His equations predicted that the universe is dynamic meaning that it is ever expanding or contracting. This discovery opposed the previously held theory that the universe was static. Einstein's equations, however, helped him to develop the general theory of relativity. In 1929, astronomer Edwin Hubble found that the universe was indeed expanding, thereby confirming Einstein's work.

While Einstein was touring much of the world speaking on his theories in the 1920s, in his own country Germany, the Nazis were gradually rising to power led by Adolf Hitler. Einstein's theories became the target of the Nazis and they would not tolerate Einstein. In 1931, the Nazi's made sure that the physicists condemned Einstein and his theories as "Jewish physics." During this time, while Einstein was still away from Germany, he learnt that the Nazis had passed a law barring all Jews from holding any official position, including teaching at universities. He also learnt that his name was on a list of assassination targets. Further, a Nazi organization had published a magazine with Einstein's picture on the cover bearing a caption "Not Yet Hanged".

Dynamic *it is the way things or people behave with each other in different situations; someone energetic*
Static *it means having no change or causing no movement; fixed in one place*

Moving to the United States

In December, 1932, Einstein left Germany forever. He took a position in the Institute for Advanced Study at Princeton, New Jersey. Physicists poured from all over to interact with Einstein. Einstein continued to work here all his life trying to bring forth a unified field theory—an all-embracing theory that would unify the forces of the universe, and in turn the laws of physics into one tight framework. Meanwhile, many European scientists threatened by the Nazis also took shelter in the United States. Some among these knew of Nazi plans to create an atomic bomb. They gave warnings to United States concerning their fears about the rising Nazi strength but for a time their words remained unheard.

Then, in summer 1939, Einstein along with another scientist Leo Szilard, was persuaded to write a letter to President Franklin D. Roosevelt. The aim of the letter was to alert President Roosevelt concerning the development of atomic bomb in Germany. President Roosevelt at last heard what the scientists had been saying for a while. It is believed that the letter became the key that led United States to undertake the development of nuclear weapons. Roosevelt met Einstein and soon the Manhattan Project was underway in the United States.

By now, Einstein had been granted permanent residency in the US in 1935. It was however, in 1940 that he became a US citizen.

Einstein now a US citizen

Suddenly, on August 6, 1945, while he was on

vacation, Einstein heard that an atomic bomb had been dropped on Hiroshima, Japan. Gravely concerned, Einstein began efforts to bring the atomic bomb under control. Then, in 1946, he formed the Emergency Committee of Atomic Scientists along with physicist Leo Szilard.

After the war, Einstein continued to work on many key aspects of the theory of general relativity including time travelling, existence of black holes and how the universe was created. During his researches, he gradually became isolated from the physics community. It was because with the development of the atomic bomb, the scientists had started working on the Quantum Theory instead of the theory of relativity. Also, during this time, Einstein had become obsessed with discovering his unified field theory.

Final Years

In the last decade of his life, Einstein withdrew from public life. He rarely travelled and often took long walks around Princeton with his close associates. Then, on April 17, 1955, while preparing a speech, Einstein suffered an abdominal aortic aneurysm and had internal bleeding. He was rushed to the hospital but he refused surgery stating that he had lived his life. The next day, April 18, Einstein died at the age of 76.

Einstein in his final years

Einstein had revolutionized the world of science. He remained a renowned scientist all his life but became the most famous scientist of the 20th century after his death.

Alexander Fleming

In 1928, Scottish bacteriologist Alexander Fleming made a chance discovery when he happened to examine an already discarded, contaminated Petri dish. He saw a mould in the solution inside the Petri dish. The mold that had contaminated the experiment contained a powerful antibiotic, penicillin. Though. Fleming is credited with discovering Penicillin but it took a decade before penicillin would turn into the wonder drug and change the 20th century.

Early Life

On August 6, 1881, Sir Alexander Fleming was born at Lochfield farm near Darvel in Ayrshire, Scotland. His father, Hugh Fleming, was a farmer and Grace Sterling was his mother. He was third of the four children. Alexander was seven years old when his father passed away. His Scottish surrounding sharpened his observation skills and appreciation of the natural world.

He attended Louden Moor School and Darvel School. He then earned a two-year scholarship to Kilmarnock Academy before moving to London where he attended the Royal Polytechnic. He spent four years working in a shipping office before entering St. Mary's Medical School, London University. He attended the medical school after his elder brother, Thomas, who worked as an oculist, suggested that he too should follow medicine as his career. Bright Alexander saw this as his opportunity and joined the medical school in 1901. At the university, he was funded by a scholarship and a legacy from his uncle. He qualified with distinction in 1906. At first, he wanted to be a surgeon but then after working

Oculist is a doctor that looks after and treats people's eyes

temporarily in the Inoculation Department at St. Mary's Medical School, he realized that his field was in Bacteriology. While there, he came and began research at St. Mary's under Sir Almroth Wright, who was a pioneer in vaccine therapy. He was awarded a gold medal in 1908 for being the top medical student at the London University. He then continued as a lecturer at the university till 1914.

In 1915, he married an Irish nurse, Sarah Marion McElroy. During World War I, he worked as a bacteriologist with the Royal Army Medical Corps. As a bacteriologist, he studied wound infection at a medical hospital in a casino in Boulogne, France.

During his stay at St. Mary's

Pioneer *someone who is the first to do or discover something*
Vaccine *it is a substance that protects the body against a disease*

There he proved that strong antiseptics on wounds did more harm than good. He suggested that the wound should be kept as clean as possible. He returned to St. Mary's in 1918. On his arrival, he was promoted as the assistant director of the inoculation department.

First Discovery

After returning from World War I, he began searching for anti-bacterial agents. He began his search after seeing numerous soldiers dying because of infected wounds. Then in 1921, Fleming discovered Lysozyme. It was an enzyme, present in body fluids such as saliva and tears, which had a mild antiseptic in it. Fleming considered the study of Lysozyme as his best work as a scientist. His work on the enzyme was significant because it helped one understand how the body fought against infection. However, this enzyme had very little or no effect on pathogenic bacteria.

The Chance Discovery in 1928

On September 28, 1928, Alexander Fleming returned to his work bench in the laboratory at

Enzyme are several proteins produced by living things which bring about certain chemical changes

St. Mary's Medical School after a vacation at his country house with his family. As he sat at his work bench he saw something unusual. Before he had left on his vacation, Fleming had piled a number of his Petri dishes to the side of the bench. He noticed that a certain culture plate had been contaminated by a fungus.

The infected culture in the petri dish

At that time he was working to discover the properties of *Staphylococci*. On a broader spectrum he was trying to find a 'wonder drug' that would prevent the infection in the wounds

Petri dish *a small, circular, shallow dish that is used for growing bacteria*
Contaminate *something unclean or impure; an infection that makes someone or something impure*
Spectrum *it is a band of coloured light as seen in a rainbow*

without harming the human body. What he found astonishing in the fungus was that the colonies of Staphylococci around the fungus had been destroyed. The farther colonies were still normal. Fleming now wondered whether he was within reach to find a wonder drug.

The Mould

Fleming then showed the contaminated culture to his former assistant Merlin Price. Price urged Fleming to further conduct studies on the fungus. Fleming then placed the fungus mould in a pure culture. Soon, he discovered that the fungus killed a number of disease killing bacteria. Then, he once again showed the mould to Price and then identified the mould as belonging to the *Penicillium* Genus. Then, after calling it "mould juice" for a few months, he named the mould Penicillin on March 7, 1928.

Fleming then observed the beneficial effect of the mould on various organisms. His observations showed him that the mould showed positive effect against several bacteria that cause scarlet fever,

Mould it is a hollow container or vessel which is used to give a particular shape to something in a molten or liquid state

pneumonia, meningitis, typhoid fever and several other bacteria caused infections and diseases.

He further tried to find out the substance in penicillin that destroyed the bacteria. Though he was unable to purify and stabilize penicillin but he did prove that it was the drug that worked as an antiseptic against a number of diseases caused by various bacteria.

Then, in 1929, Fleming published his discovery in the *British Journal of Experimental Pathology*. But little attention was paid to his article. Though disappointed with response to his article Fleming continued with his experiments on Penicillin.

Could this be the "wonder drug"? Fleming, himself was not certain about it though he saw the potential of the drug.

Twelve Years Later

Though no matter what Fleming did he wasn't able to produce the drug in quantity. Also as its action was rather slow Fleming thought that the drug may not be important in treating humans. His further tests also remained inconclusive. Also as he wasn't a chemist he could not further refine penicillin which had been used. After a few years, Fleming then gave up on penicillin.

Then in 1940, the second year of World War II, two scientists at Oxford University started researching on promising projects in bacteriology. Then, Australian Pathologist Howard Florey and British Biochemist Ernst Chain began working with penicillin. Using new chemical techniques, these two were able to produce a brown powder that kept its antibacterial power for more than a few days. As they continued to experiment with the powder they found it to be safe.

As World War II was underway, the duo started making mass production of Penicillin. The use of penicillin during the world war saved the lives of many soldiers.

Recognition

Though Fleming had discovered penicillin, it were Florey and Chain who had converted it into a usable product. For their contribution to medicine, Fleming, Florey and Chain were jointly awarded the 1945 Nobel Prize in Physiology or Medicine. Nonetheless, it was Fleming's chance discovery that had changed the world of medicine. He is therefore credited with the discovery of penicillin.

Winning the Noble Prize in 1945

Penicillin has cemented Fleming's name in medical history. A few years before he received the Nobel Prize, Fleming was knighted. Later, it was in 1949 that his first wife passed away. Then, in 1953,

Fleming married Greek microbiologist Amalia Coutsouris-Voureka. In the last decade of his life, Fleming remained among the best known scientist of his time. He passed away in 1955 after a heart attack.

Fleming would always be known as the discoverer of the "wonder drug" penicillin.

Thomas Alva Edison

Thomas Edison is the quintessential American inventor. He invented the phonograph, the transmitter for the telephone speaker, an improved light bulb, and key elements of motion-picture apparatus, along with numerous other inventions. The development of the world's first industrial research laboratory also goes to his credit.

Early Life

Thomas Alva Edison was born on February 11, 1847, in Milan, Ohio. He was the youngest of his parents, Samuel and Nancy Edison's, seven children. His father had escaped from Canada and his mother was a skilled school teacher. His mother had a major influence in Thomas' early life. Early in his life, Thomas suffered from scarlet fever. Though he recovered but he developed difficulty in hearing that left him nearly deaf as an adult.

In 1854, when Thomas was seven years old, the family moved to Port Huron, Michigan. Here, for the first time, Edison attended a public school though only for 12 weeks. Thomas was a hyperactive child and his constant distraction made his teacher call him a "difficult" child. Tired of the teacher's complaints, Thomas' mother pulled him out of the school and started home tutoring him. As an 11 year old, Thomas showed a

Young Edison

voracious appetite for knowledge, and he started reading books on a wide range of subjects. In the process of reading books, Edison started teaching himself and began learning independently. His believe in self improvement became his motto for life.

Beginning of a Lifelong Career

At age 12, Edison decided to put all his education to use. He, therefore, began convincing his parents to let him sell newspapers to passengers along the Grand Trunk Railroad line. It was some time before his parents agreed. Exploiting his access to the news bulletins teletyped to the station office each day, Edison began publishing the *Grand Trunk Herald*, his own newspaper. The newspaper became a hit with the passengers. This venture also became the first among the many entrepreneurial undertakings Edison would start during his lifetime.

During this time, Edison also used his access to the railroad to conduct chemical experiments in a small laboratory which he had set up inside a train

Voracious eating or wanting to eat a large quantity of food

baggage car. One day when he was conducting some experiments, a chemical fire started inside the carriage and quickly the fire spread. Due to the efforts of the conductor, no terrible incident took place. However, the conductor did struck Edison on the side of the head which furthered his hearing loss. After this incident, Edison was kicked off the train and he had to sell his newspapers at various stations along the train route.

Things took a different turn when another incident changed the course of his life. During this time, Edison was still working for the railroad. The incident involved, Edison saving the life of a three-year-old from being run over by an errant train. Edison was greatly praised and the child's grateful father rewarded Edison by teaching him how to operate a telegraph. At 15, Edison had learnt so much that he could be easily employed as a telegraph operator. Then, for the next five years, Edison continued to travel throughout the Midwest as a telegrapher. Even then, he managed to study and experiment with telegraph technology. Soon, he became familiar with the electrical science.

Errant *moving aimlessly looking for adventure; not following or behaving in the accepted manner*

Then, in 1866, at age 19, Edison moved to Louisville, Kentucky and started working for *The Associated Press*. After his shift was over, he continued to experiment. During this time, he continued to examine and experiment and prove things to himself. Initially, Edison excelled at his telegraph job but as improvements were made in the way telegraphs were sent by using sound, the improvements proved a disadvantage for Edison. He gradually had less employment opportunities.

In 1868, Edison returned home. At home, he found his mother mentally ill and learnt that his father had no work. Edison family was almost poverty stricken. In order to improve the condition of the family, Edison moved to Boston. There he started working for the Western Union Company. At the time, Boston was America's center for science and culture, and Edison couldn't have been at a better place. In his spare time, he continued to conduct his experiments. Then, he designed and patented an electronic voting recorder that could quickly tally the votes after an election. However, the lawmakers did not like the experiment as they did not want that the votes be quickly tallied.

Edison the Inventor

In 1869, Edison moved to New York City. It was here that he developed his first invention. It was an improved stock ticker, the Universal Stock Printer, which synchronized several stock tickers' transactions. Then, only at 22 years of age, Edison sold the rights of his invention for $40,000. With his first success, Edison quit his work as a telegrapher and devoted himself to inventing.

Thomas Edison, in 1870, set up his first laboratory and manufacturing facility in Newark, New Jersey. He employed several machinists to help him with his work. As he was an independent entrepreneur, Edison developed many partnerships and made his products that made the highest bid. Mostly, he made products for Western Union Telegraph Company. In one instance, Edison devised for Western Union the quadruplex telegraph, which was capable of transmitting two signals in two different directions on the same wire. However, railroad tycoon Jay Gould paid Edison more than $100,000 in cash, bonds and stocks and snatched the product from Western Union followed by a lawsuit.

Synchronized *to do something at the same time as something else*
Laboratory *a room in a school or college building where scientific research and experiments take place*

Edison was now financially prosperous. Then, in 1871, Edison married 16 year old Mary Stilwell. They had a thirteen year long marriage and they had three children, Marion, Thomas and William. Things again changed for Edison when Mary died of a suspected brain tumour at the age of 29 in 1884.

By the early 1870s, Thomas Edison had become well known. In 1876, he moved to Menlo Park, New Jersey and there he built an independent industrial research facility which included machine shops and laboratories. In December 1877, Edison developed a tin foil phonograph which recorded sound.

It was the first machine that could record and reproduce sound created by a sensation and brought Edison international fame. Edison toured the country with the tin foil phonograph, and was even invited to the White House to demonstrate its working to President Rutherford B. Hayes in April 1878.

In his laboratory

World's Great Inventors

The Evolution of Light

Edison remained busy during the 1880s. Soon, he started working on his greatest challenge, the development of a practical incandescent, electric light. The idea of electric lighting was not new, and a number of people had worked on it, and had even developed various forms of electric lighting. But no one so far had been able to develop what was remotely practical for home use. Edison's greatest achievement lay in the fact that he was able to make incandescent light practical, safe, and economical.

Once he had got the patent for the light bulb in 1880, Edison began developing a company that would provide electricity and light up the world. In the same year, he founded the Edison Illuminating Company—the first investor-owned electric utility. The following year, Edison devoted his

Edison with his Tin foil phonograph

Incandescent *something which gives out light after it has been heated*

time to establish facilities in cities where electrical systems were being installed.

In 1882, something revolutionary happened. After one and a half years of work, Edison achieved success when an incandescent lamp with a filament of carbonized sewing thread burned for thirteen and a half hours. The first public demonstration of the Edison's incandescent lighting system took place in December 1879, when the Menlo Park laboratory complex was electrically lighted. Edison spent the next several years creating the electric industry.

Menlo Park Laboratory

Mina Miller

That year, the first commercial power station located on Pearl Street provided 110 volts of electrical power and light to 59 customers in lower Manhattan. The electric age had begun. In 1886 Edison married Mina Miller who was 19 years his junior. In 1887, Edison set up an industrial research laboratory in West Orange, New Jersey. The laboratory was less than a mile from his home and it consisted of five buildings. It served as the primary research laboratory for Edison lighting companies.

The large size of the laboratory allowed Edison to work on a number of projects at any given time. Facilities were added to the laboratory or modified to meet Edison's changing needs as he continued to work here till his death in 1931. Over the years, factories were built around the laboratory to manufacture Edison inventions. The entire laboratory and factory complex eventually covered about twenty acres and employed around 10,000 people during World War I.

Meanwhile, the success of his electric light had taken Edison to new heights of fame and wealth, as electricity spread around the world. Edison's various electric companies continued to grow until in 1889 when they were combined to form the Edison General Electric. Though the company was named after him but Edison never controlled the company. So, there were partnerships with investment bankers to acquire capital to develop the incandescent lighting industry. It was later in 1892 that the company was renamed as simply General Electric.

Edison spent a majority of his time at West Orange supervising the development of lighting technology and power systems. It was here that he started developing the alkaline battery and the motion picture camera.

Like his previous inventions, Edison developed a complete system for a working motion picture camera. His work in motion pictures was pioneering and original. Further over many years, more people added to it to improve the motion pictures. By the late 1890s, a thriving new industry of motion pictures had been firmly established, and by 1918 the industry had become so competitive that Edison got out of the movie business all together.

Edison General Electric

Becoming an Industrialist and a Business Manager

Over the next few decades, Edison transformed from being an inventor to being an industrialist and a business manager. Edison found that the laboratory in West Orange was too large to be properly managed. He also realised that he was not very successful here unlike his previous laboratory. He also saw that he worked best with a handful of assistants instead of working with a number of mathematicians and scientists.

However, not all that he invented was a success. But he also had the potential to turn a near failure into a success. During the 1890s, his magnetic iron-ore processing plant in northern New Jersey proved to be a failure. He, however, managed to convert it into a better method for producing cement. As the automobile industry grew, Edison worked on developing a suitable storage battery to power an electric car. Though the automobiles continued to be driven by gasoline but in 1921, Edison designed a battery for the self-starter on the Model T for Henry Ford. The system was used extensively in the auto industry.

During World War I, the US government asked Thomas Edison to head the Naval Consulting Board, which examined inventions submitted for military use. Edison worked on several projects including submarine detectors and gun-location techniques, limiting his examinations to only defensive weapons.

By the end of the 1920s Thomas Edison was in his 80s and it was then that he had applied for the last of his 1,093 U.S. patents. It was for an apparatus that held objects during the electroplating process.

By now, Edison and his wife, Mina, had started spending a majority of their time at their winter retreat in Fort Myers, Florida. Here, he befriended automobile tycoon Henry Ford. Together they worked on several projects. Their projects ranged from electric trains to finding a domestic source for natural rubber.

Edison with Henry Ford

Apparatus *it is a group of tools or equipments that are used to do a particular task*

In 1928, in recognition of his lifelong achievements, the United States Congress voted Edison a special Medal of Honor. In 1929, the nation celebrated the golden jubilee of the incandescent light.

A Great Life Comes to an End

During the last two years of his life, Edison used to fall ill more often. He was unable to spend a lot of time in the laboratory and needed to rest. On October 18, 1931, Thomas Edison died of complications arising from diabetes at his home, Glenmont, in West Orange, New Jersey. He was 84 years old. When the news of his death became known, several corporations around the world dimmed or briefly turned off their lights to commemorate his passing. Edison's success was a classical rag to riches story. He is considered one of the leading American businessmen. He brought about America's first technological revolution and set the stage for the modern electric world.

The Wright Brothers

Wilbur and Orville Wright were brothers and inventors of the world's first successful airplane. They are considered the fathers of modern aviation. Their greatest achievement was in developing the three axis control. It was something that helped the pilot to control and steer the aircraft efficiently while maintaining the equilibrium of the aircraft. After Wilber had passed away, Orville began developing technology for the United States army.

Early Life

Wilbur Wright was born on April 16, 1867, near Millville, Indiana and Orville Wright was born on August 19, 1871 in Dayton, Ohio. Wilbur was the middle child among five children while Orville was his younger brother. Susan Catherine Koerner was their mother and Milton Wright, a bishop in the Church of the United Brethren in Christ was their father. It was after the birth of Wilbur that the family moved to Dayton, Ohio.

Wilbur was a bright student and he excelled in his studies at school. He had a strong personality and he wanted to study at Yale University after he had completed school. Orville, on the other hand, was a mischievous and curious boy. His family, however, always encouraged him and let his intellect develop.

Orville wrote in his memoirs, "We were lucky enough to grow up in an environment where there was always much encouragement to children to pursue intellectual interests; to investigate whatever aroused curiosity."

Their father, Milton Wright, travelled often for his church work and brought something for his children. During one of his trips in 1878, Milton Wright brought home a toy helicopter for his boys. The toy based on an invention by French aeronautical pioneer Alphonse Pénaud, was made of cork, bamboo and paper. A rubber band was used to twirl its twin blades. When Orville and Wilbur saw the toy, they were fascinated and it was then that their life long passion for aeronautics developed.

In 1881, the Wright family moved to Richmond, Indiana. While in Richmond, Orville developed a love of kites, and he began making his own kites at home. It was also here that Wilbur's dreams of attending Yale University were shattered. In the year 1886-87, Wilbur suffered a terrible accident that changed the course of his life. He got badly injured in an ice hockey match when during the game the hockey stick of another player hit him in the face. Though Wilbur recovered but he became depressed. He did not receive his high school diploma and refused to attend college. He retreated towards home. During this time, he read a number of books and also looked after his ailing mother.

Aeronautics *it is the science that deals with the making and flying of aircrafts*

Then, in 1887 the family once again moved back to Ohio, where Orville enrolled at Dayton Central High School. He, however, was more interested to know what was happening outside the classroom than what was happening inside. It was no surprise when he dropped out in his junior year of high school, and opened a print shop. He had worked in a print shop over summer, and now began designed his own printing press. On March 1, 1889 he began publishing the *West Side News*, a weekly paper for West Dayton. Wilbur was the paper's editor and Orville became the publisher. The brothers were successfull in their venture and prospered.

In the same year, tragedy struck the Wright family. Orville's mother, Susan Catherine Koerner Wright, died after a long bout of tuberculosis. After their mother had passed away, their sister

Wright Brothers

Katherine started looking after the household. It was during this time that the bond between the three siblings strengthened further and remained so throughout their lives.

The Bicycle Shop

After their mother's death, Orville and his brother dedicated themselves to another shared interest, bicycles. It was because a new, safer design of the bicycle had set off a bicycle craze across the country. The Wright Brothers did not want to let go of this opportunity. So, they opened a bicycle shop in 1892 meant for selling and fixing bikes. The brothers were successful and in 1896 they started manufacturing a bicycle which they had designed. Orville invented a self-oiling wheel hub for their popular bikes. Soon, they were selling, repairing, designing and manufacturing their own line of hand-built, made-to-order bicycles. They first manufactured the Van Cleve and the Wright Special, and later the less expensive St Clair. The Wright Brothers kept their bicycle shop until 1907. The profits made through the shop allowed them to successfully fund their flight research. These ventures also showed their business sense and originality.

Bicycle designed & manufactured by the Wright Brothers

Inventing the Airplane

Always curious about the new developments in aeronautics, Orville and Wilbur followed the latest flying news. They especially closely followed the research of famous German aviator Otto Lilienthal. It was then that they realized that manned flight was possible. So, Wilbur started reading all he could to find about the science of aviation. Then, one day

World's Great Inventors

they learnt that Otto Lilienthal had died in a glider crash. The Wright Brothers were by now convinced and decided to start their own experiments with flight. The brothers were determined to develop their own work, so they headed to Kitty Hawk, North Carolina, where strong winds provided ideal conditions to fly.

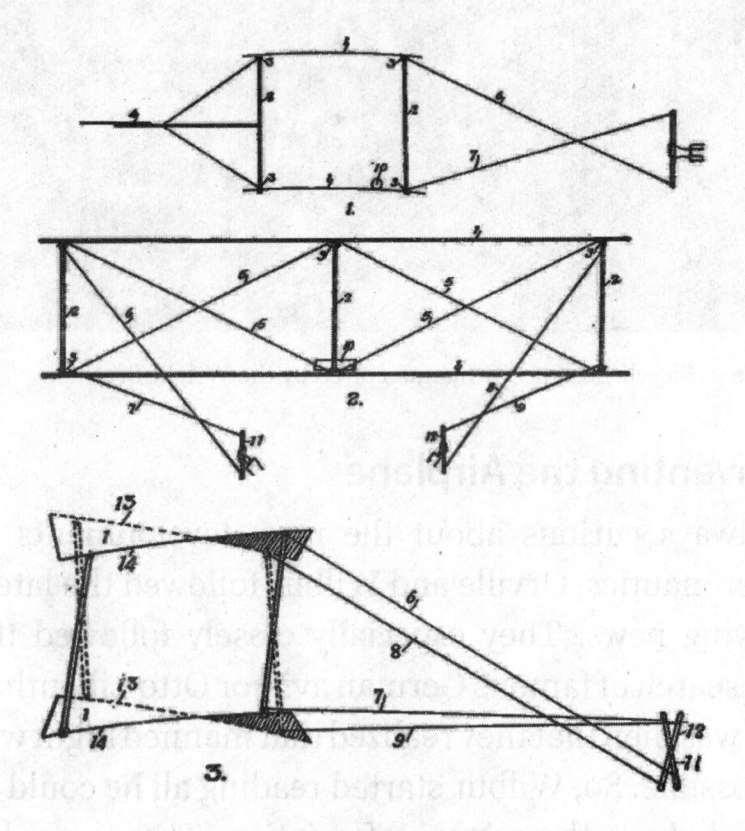

Designs of an aircraft

Glider *it is an engine aircraft that is used to fly from a higher to a lower level under the force of the air currents and gravity*

Orville and Wilbur started experimenting with wings. Wilbur Wright thought of a ideal solution to the problem of flight. He described it as "a simple system that twisted, or warped the wings of a biplane, causing it to roll right and left." Wilbur and Orville then started working to find out how to design wings for flight. They had realized that so far no one has been able to develop a system to control flight while the plane was in the air. Then, they observed that the birds angled their wings to balance and control their bodies during flight. The brothers coined the concept called "wing warping" and utilized it to develop a moveable rudder. The brothers had managed to make a design that had eluded all those who came before them.

The concept of "wing warping" allowed the pilot to control the roll of the plane ie the horizontal movement of the plane by raising or lowering the flaps located along the plane's wingtips. For instance, if one raised a flap and lowered the other, it would turn the plane. Based on this concept the brothers made a glider and tested it. However, the glider did not work well in the beginning. The brothers, however, continued to make

Rudder is a vertical blade in a vessel used to change the vessel's direction when it is moving

improvements and gradually learnt to control the glider while it was in flight. Now they needed an airplane that had not only the control of the wings but also motorized power. Soon they made an airplane with had a 4 cylinder, 12 horsepower gasoline engine weighing 200 pounds. They began their testing in no time.

One of the planes made by Wright Brothers

On December 17, 1903, the Wright Brothers tasted success. They succeeded in flying the first free, controlled flight of a power-driven, heavier than airplane. Orville Wright made four flights that day. His first flight at 10:36 A.M. on Kill Devil Hill

Engine *is a part of a vehicle or machine that uses energy to make the vehicle move or the machine work*

lasted for 12 seconds and the plane flew for 120 feet. The brothers were excited and they continued to conduct more flights that day. But it was the fourth flight made by Wilbur that lasted for 59 seconds and the plane flew 852 feet. The Wright Brothers had been successful. Thus the era of manned flight had begun. After this success, the brothers continued to improve their airplane.

Fame

The Wright Brothers, however, soon realized that not everyone appreciated their success. Many in the press, along with flight experts, were hesitant to believe the brother's claims. It was also because a number of further experiments had failed. Due to this, even the United States government refused to back them. Then, Wilbur set out for Europe in 1908, where he hoped that they would have more success convincing the public and sell their airplanes. In France, Wilbur found a more encouraging audience. He made several public demonstrations and even gave rides to officials, journalists and statesmen.

Meanwhile, Orville headed to Washington, D.C. where he demonstrated their flying machine in the hope of winning government and army contracts. Then, in July 1909, Orville completed the demonstration flights for the United States Army, who demanded that they built a passenger seat in the plane. When that was done, the Wright Brothers sold the plane for $30,000.

A manned airplane

Their extraordinary success led to contracts both in Europe and the United States. Soon, the Wright Brothers had become wealthy business owners.

They started building a grand family home in Dayton, a place where they had spent much of their childhood.

Wilbur and Orville always shared the credit or their innovations. Behind the scenes, however, one could see division of labour.

Then, on May 25, 1910, Orville flew for six minutes with his brother Wilbur. It would be the first and the only flight that the brothers would make together. The same day, Orville also took his 82 year old father, Milton Wright, on his maiden and only flight.

In 1912, after Wilbur passed away, Orville took over the presidency of the Wright Company. Unlike his brother, he did not have a business sense and therefore, he sold the company in 1915. He built himself an aeronautics laboratory, and returned to what he and his brother were best at: inventing. He also stayed active in the public eye as he promoted aeronautics, continued to invent and wrote about his first historic flight. On April 8, 1930, Orville Wright received the first Daniel Guggenheim Medal, awarded for his "great achievements in aeronautics."

Death and Legacy

Wilbur Wright fell ill on a trip to Boston in April 1912. He was diagnosed with typhoid fever. He was unable to recover and he died on May 30 at his family home in Dayton, Ohio.

Milton Wright, his father, wrote in his diary, "A short life, full of consequences. An unfailing intellect, imperturbable temper, great self-reliance and as great a modesty, seeing the right clearly, pursuing it steadfastly, he lived and died."

Orville, however, after his brother's death spent the last three decades of his life serving on boards and committees related to aeronautics, including the National Advisory Committee for Aeronautics (NACA), which was a predecessor to NASA. Neither of the brothers had married and Orville greatly disapproved of his sister Katherine's choice in marriage.

Orville died on January 30, 1948, after a second heart attack. He is buried at the Wright family plot in Dayton, Ohio. He was 76 years old.

Charles Babbage

Charles Babbage (1791-1871) is widely regarded as the first computer pioneer and a figure given the greatest respect in the history of computing. His conception of the Analytical Engine in 1834 is considered his greatest achievement and a startling intellectual feat of the nineteenth century. The design of the Analytical Engine has features of modern computers. It was, however, only in the 1930s and 40s that the work of Babbage became known and was put into use.

Early Life

Charles Babbage was born on December 26, 1791 in Walworth, Surrey. He was one of the four children born to banker Benjamin Babbage and Elizabeth Teape.

He attended a number of schools though he often remained ill. Then after a bout of fever, he was mainly home tutored. After completing his studies, he attended Trinity College, Cambridge in 1810. It was here that his fascination with mathematics grew. Later, he graduated from Peterhouse in 1814 and received an MA in 1817. Till 1828, he stayed at Devonshire Street in London before his move to 1 Dorset Street, Manchester Square, London. Charles Babbage stayed here till his death. He was elected a fellow of the Royal Society in 1816 and was even hired by the Royal Institute to present a lecture on Calculus. He even occupied the Lucasian Chair of Mathematics at Cambridge University from 1828 to 1839.

Between 1813 and 1868, Babbage published six books along with ninety papers. His talents and interests were wide ranging though Babbage is mostly known for his pioneering work on automatic calculating engines. His engines were of two kinds: Difference Engines and Analytical Engines. The engines designed by Babbage were monumental in their concept, size and complexity.

Marriage and Family

On July 25, 1814, Babbage married Georgiana Whitmore at St. Michael's Church in Teignmouth, Devon. Charles and Georgiana had eight children, but only four — Benjamin Herschel, Georgiana Whitmore, Dugald Bromhead and Henry Prevost — survived childhood. Charles' wife Georgiana died in Worcester on September 1, 1827, the same year as his father, their second son and their newborn son Alexander.

His youngest son, Henry Prevost Babbage created six working Difference Engines based on his father's designs, one of these engines were sent to the Harvard University.

His Fascination with Printed Tables

Babbage was fascinated by printed tables and he had a collection of about 300 volumes of printed

Monumental something important; massive in structure or deed

tables in his possession. He could easily find the errors in these tables and these errors led him to design a device that could eliminate the errors present in the mathematical tables.

During the 17th and 18th centuries several attempts had been made to build devices that would aid in mathematical calculations. Devices built by early pioneers including Schickard, Pascal and Leibniz could not be used in daily routine and were thus generally ignored. All this while, mathematical tables were used to perform calculations which were laborious and not always accurate.

These tables, moreover, were prone to three basic kinds of errors. These errors included errors of calculation (all calculations at that time were done by human beings), errors of transcription (these errors occurred when the results were copied to give them to the printer) and thirdly there were errors of typesetting and printing.

Designing the Difference Engine No. 1

His machines were the first mechanical engines. In 1821, Babbage began developing a device that could

Eliminate to get rid of; remove something
Transcription it is the process where something is represented by writing about it or printing it

not only calculate automatically without creating errors but also print the results without any error. Babbage called this device a Difference Engine because the device used the mathematical principle of finite differences to calculate. The advantage of using this method was that it eliminated the use of multiplication and division while calculating polynomials. The Difference Engine only used addition to calculate.

Difference Engine No. 1

Babbage, however, did not build his machine. It was because the Victorian mechanical engineering

Finite *something which is measurable; has boundaries and limitations*
Polynomial *it is an algebraic expression. It is depicted by more than one group of numbers or letters which are joined by + or -*

was not sufficiently developed to produce the numerous parts of the machine on a vast scale.

The design of Difference Engine No. 1 if completed required an estimated 25,000 parts which amounted to about 15 tonnes. A complete engine would have stood eight feet in height, seven foot long and three foot in depth. Babbage did however hire Joseph Clement, a skilled toolmaker and draughtsman, to build the Engine. He managed to make one complete portion of the engine in 1832 which is now a celebrated icon of the history of computing. It is the oldest surviving automatic calculator of the time. Baggage was provided a government funding of £17,500 but even when nothing substantial was built, the funding stopped. Thus, in 1833, the work on the engine came to a halt.

The Analytical Engine

Then, in 1834 though the Difference Engine remained incomplete Babbage had thought of a new device called the Analytical Engine. This machine, more technically advanced, worked on the same

Draughtsman is a person who draws plans of structures or someone who writes legal and official documents

Analytical Engine

principle on which the modern computers work. Like his Difference Engines, Babbage never got to completely build the Analytical Engine and only a few partially complete assemblies were built. By 1840, the Analytical Engine remained largely incomplete.

The designs for the Analytical Engine include features of a modern computer. It performed mathematical calculations using punching cards that contained instructions to perform calculations.

Analytical *a process that calls for analysis; a method of observing the various parts of a device in order to understand the device*

It has a 'store' where numbers and their results were stored and a separate section (mill) where arithmetic processing took place. The separate 'store' (memory) and 'mill' (central processor) are essential features of modern electronic computers. The Analytical Engine could repeat the same sequence of operations a number of times and was even capable of automatically performing different operations depending on the result of a calculation.

The Analytical Engine was not only automatic, it could be used for general purpose as well. It means that the device could be 'programmed' by the user to execute repertoire instructions in any required order. The engine could find the value of almost any algebraic function. Charles Babbage continued to improve the Analytical Engine until his death.

Building Difference Engine No. 2

Again in 1847, Babbage started building Difference Engine No. 2. This machine was simple compared to the Analytical Engine. The design of Difference Engine No.2 required less parts then Difference Engine No.1 for doing the same amount of

Repertoire *includes all the plays and songs that a performer knows and can perform*

computing power. Babbage made no attempt to construct Difference Engine No. 2 like he did with Difference Engine No. 1.

Difference Engine No. 2

His Difference Engines, however, were automatic and they did not require being operated. They were also the first designs to use mathematical rules in a device though they were not general purpose machines. Moreover, the numbers added to the device could be done only in a particular sequence.

It was only in 1985 that due to a project at the Science Museum, the complete Babbage Engine was built to see if the model was practical at all. The Engine chosen was Babbage's Difference Engine No. 2. The calculating section of the Engine, which weighed 2.6 tonnes with 4,000 separate parts, was completed and became fully functional in November 1991, a month before the 200th birth anniversary of Charles Babbage.

The calculating section of Difference Engine No. 2, when it was made, had 4,000 moving parts (excluding the printing mechanism) and weighed about 2.6 tonnes. It was seven feet high, eleven feet long and eighteen inches in depth. It also became the first full sized Babbage calculating engine to be completed.

Praise for his Analytical Engine

In 1842, an Italian mathematician, Louis Menebrea, published a memoir in French on the Analytical Engine. Babbage was delighted with the interest shown in his project and appointed Ada Lovelace to act as a translator for the article.

Ada added a series of in depth notes showing the amount of understanding she had of Babbage's work. Babbage, however, never made an attempt to build the Analytical Engine. He instead continued to work on simpler and cheaper methods of manufacturing the parts of the device. After his death, his work was generally lost as no one tried to do work on it.

Later Life and Death

Baggage apart from designing various parts for his engines, took interest in code breaking and also in the field of philosophy. He even campaigned to bring about reforms in British science. During his life he continued to work in different intellectual fields and was well-known despite his Difference and Analytical Engines. He, however, remained known for his Difference and Analytical Engines and is called 'the father of computing'.

Charles Babbage died in his London home on October 18, 1871.

Reform *is to make things better; improving the system, law or an organization by making suitable changes*
Code *a set of symbols used to send messages; a set of principles or laws of a state or country*

Rudolf Diesel

Rudolf Christian Karl Diesel was a German inventor and a mechanical engineer. He is famous for inventing the internal combustion engine which is now named after him as the 'Diesel Engine'. He was also a linguist, a theorist and a connoisseur of arts.

Early Life

Rudolf Diesel was born on March 18, 1858 in Paris, France. His parents Theodor and Elise Diesel were Bavarian immigrants who lived in Paris. He was the second of the three children of his parents. Diesel spent his early childhood in France. However, when the Franco-German War broke out in 1870, the Diesels went to London, England. After a brief stay in London, Rudolf Diesel was sent to Augsberg, his father's native town in Germany to stay with his aunt and uncle and to complete his schooling. After completing his schooling in 1873, Diesel went to the Munich Polytechnic in 1975. Here, he had an excellent record as an engineer.

Work After Graduation

When he had completed his graduation in 1880, a year later than he should have as he fell grievously ill, he returned to Paris. Here, Diesel was employed as a refrigerator engineer at Linde Refrigeration Enterprises. It was a company owned by his former Munich professor, Carl von Linde. Due to his hard work and intelligence, Diesel became the director

Immigrant *is a person who goes to live in another country permanently*
Grievously *causing tremendous grief and sorrow*

of the company a year later. While working at the Enterprises, Diesel gained several patents both in France and Germany.

In 1890, Diesel moved to Berlin with his wife and three children and took over the management of the Linde corporate and research department. Now, he was not allowed to use the patents he had acquired as an employee of the Linde enterprises, to use for his own purposes. Due to this, he began thinking beyond refrigeration.

So, he began working on designing his own distinctive engine. But before he designed his internal combustion engine, he first began by building the steam engine. Besides the steam engine, he also built a solar-powered air engine. His early research into fuel efficiency led him to build a "steam engine" using ammonia vapour. While he was conducting his tests, the engine exploded with fatal consequences. Diesel was hospitalized for many months. Due to this accident, he suffered from a great deal of ill health and had eyesight problems in later life.

Combustion *a process of burning; a rapid chemical process that produces heat and light*
Corporate *belonging to a corporation*
Efficiency *is the ability or quality to do a specific work with minimum expenditure of time and money*
Fatal *something that has the capacity to cause death*

Marriage and Family

In 1883, Rudolf Diesel returned to Paris and here in 1885 established his own shop-laboratory in Paris. In Paris, he also became a connoisseur of the fine arts and an internationalist. During this time, he also married Martha Flasche. They had three children together—Eugen, Hedi and Rudolf Jr. In 1885, Rudolf began to pursue his life long dream and began working on designing his engine full time. Even when he moved to Berlin and began working again for Linde Enterprises, he pursued to make his engine design.

Rudolf Diesel with his family

Pursuing his Dream

After he had recovered, Diesel began designing an engine which was based on the Carnot Cycle. Then, in 1983, he came to know about Karl Benz's engine for the motor car had received a patent. Soon after,

Connoisseur *is an expert who has ample knowledge of a particular field and can judge matters which concern that field*

Diesel published a book in German titled, "Theory and design of a rational thermal engine to replace the steam engine and the combustion engines known today". This treatise formed the basis of his work. Further, he began developing an engine based on his own design. In time, he had designed his own engine and also obtained a patent for his design.

He had based his engine on maximum fuel efficiency for he knew that the steam engine wasted about 90% of the energy available in the fuel. In the engine that he had designed, fuel was injected at the end of compression. Also, the high temperature caused by compression ignited the fuel inside the engine. Diesel also managed to build a working model of the engine based on his theory and design. The engine that he designed is now known after his name as the Diesel Engine.

Then from 1893-1897, Diesel worked for Heinrich von Buz at MAN AG, an engine factory in Augsburg, Germany. Here, Heinrich von Buz gave Diesel the opportunity to test and develop his ideas. Soon, he obtained patents for his design in Germany and

Treatise *is a long and details writing about or on something*
Compression *to squeeze or press something, sometimes forcefully, into a smaller place*
Ignite *to set something on fire*

also in USA. He made the first working model of his engine in 1893 which had 26% efficiency. It was double the efficiency of the steam engine. In 1897, the first diesel engine suitable for practical use worked at a remarkable efficiency of 75%. Interestingly, the diesel engine can also run on cheaper fuel. The greatest achievement for Rudolf Diesel and his engine came in 1900 at the Paris Exposition where the diesel engine took the Grand Prix. The engine was fueled with 100% peanut oil. It must be noted that Diesel saw biomass fuel as the real future of his engine. He wanted to provide farmers and small industries the means to produce their own fuel.

Model of diesel engine

After Diesel's death, the diesel engine underwent several transformations and soon replaced the steam engine in many of its applications.

Biomass refers to organic matter taken from plants and which can be used as fuel; the number and weight of plants and animals in a given area

However, the diesel engine wasn't used in aviation as it required a heavier and strong construction compared to a gasoline engine. However, the diesel engine was widely used in submarines, ships and even, though a bit later, in locomotives and automobiles. Recently, diesel engines have been redesigned for usage in aircrafts.

Mystery Surrounding his Death

On the evening of September 29, 1913, Rudolf Diesel took a ship, SS Dresden, to cross the English Channel from Antwerp, Belgium to Harwich, England. He had his dinner on board the ship and then retired to his cabin at about 10PM. Before he returned to his cabin, he left word that he must be called the next morning at 6:15 AM. But next morning, during a roll call he was not found in his room. He had not slept on his bed and all his belongings were in the room. But he himself had disappeared. A thorough search of the ship took place but he remained missing. 10 days later, a corpse was found in the water off the Dutch coast. His son, Eugen Diesel, identified the corpse as that of his father after identifying the contents of the

Locomotive is an engine that pulls a train

man's pocket. It remained opened to speculation whether it was a suicide or a murder. However, the body wasn't buried and was returned to the sea for it was badly decomposed.

A year later, World War I broke out. Meanwhile, there was some speculation regarding the cause of his death. As his body was returned to the sea, Rudolf Diesel has no known grave. Only a simple carved piece of rock in the Rudolf Diesel Memorial Grove in Augsburg, Germany and the magnificient musemum in the M.A.N. (MAN AG) factory in Augsburg, exist as a direct memorial to one of the finest engineers the world.

JAMES WATT

James watt was a Scottish inventor who made tremendous improvements to the already existing steam engine. He was a sick child and youth but he brushed away his physical ailments to become the most important inventors in world history. The improvements that he made became fundamental to the changes that took place during the Industrial Revolution in England.

Early Beginnings

James Watt was of a humble lineage born in Greenock, Scotland on January 19, 1736. Greenock was a small fishing town which grew to become a busy town with a fleet of steamships during Watt's lifetime. His father was a shipwright, ship owner and contractor, and he also served as the town's chief baillie. His mother, Agnes Muirhead was from a distinguished family and well educated. Thomas Watt, his grandfather, was a well-known mathematician and teacher along with being a baillie to the Baron of Cartsburn.

Mechanical Mind

James Watt was an intelligent child but he used to often fall ill. Initially, he was taught at home by his mother. Later, he joined Greenock Grammar School but his ill health did not permit him to attend school regularly. So, once again his mother began teaching him. From the beginning, Watt showed a great interest towards mathematics. He also used to wander to his father's carpenter bench. Seeing the tools on his father's bench made him familiar with their use and this was where he

Shipwright *a person, especially a carpenter who builds and repairs ships*
Baillie *was a local civic officer responsible for maintaining jurisdiction, equivalent to a magistrate*

learnt the basics of engineering and tool making from his father.

While he was still very young, Watt began solving geometrical problems on his own. He also started experimenting with his mother's tea kettle, trying to understand the nature of steam.

As he grew up, his skills in the field of mathematics developed further. In his spare time, he made sketches with pencil, carved or went to his father's work bench and worked at the bench with wood and metal. He made many original pieces of mechanism, and a few beautiful models. He liked to repair nautical instruments. Among other pieces of apparatus made by Watt was a very fine barrel organ. As he grew up, his interest towards reading increased. He read a lot and found something to interest him in each book.

Apprenticeships

When Watt was eighteen years of age, he was sent to Glasgow to stay with his mother's relatives, and to learn the trade of a mathematical instrument maker. In no time he learnt all he had to from the

Nautical related to sailors, ships and navigation

mechanic he was apprenticed to and even outgrew him in terms of knowledge. It was then that a friend and professor at the University of Glasgow, Doctor Dick advised that he should go to London. James Watt moved to London in June 1755. Here, he began working for John Morgan, in Cornhill, for twenty guineas a week. But only a year had gone by when he was compelled to return home due to serious illness.

When he had recovered from his illness, James Watt returned to Glasgow in 1756. However, as he had been unable to complete his apprenticeship, he was prohibited by the guilds, or trades unions, to open a mechanical repair shop in Glasgow. Though the town of Glasgow had no mathematical instrument maker yet he was unable to open his shop. It was during this time that Doctor Dick came to his aid, and employed him to repair the astronomical apparatus that had come to the University. Watt couldn't have asked for more. He remained at the university till 1760, when he was allowed to open a mechanic shop in the city. Watt even worked briefly as a civil engineer though he always remained interested in mechanics. In his

Guinea was an old English gold coin

spare time, he made musical instruments and even made improvements in the construction of organs.

In 1764, Watt married his cousin Margaret (Peggy) Miller. Together, they had five children. She, however, died during childbirth in 1772. Watt remarried in 1777 to Ann MacGregor. They had two children together. In 1832, Ann too passed away.

Newcomen Steam Engine

While working at the University of Glasgow, Watt befriended the professors there. It was through them in 1763 that he came to know about the Newcomen steam engine. The university had a model of the steam engine and it was given to Watt for repairs. The Newcomen steam engine was used for pumping water from mines. He then began experimenting with steam though he had never seen an operating steam engine.

While Watt was given the steam engine to repair, Doctor Robison, who was a student at the University, and had befriended James Watt, used to come to his shop often. It was Robison who introduced Watt to the concept of steam engine.

It was he who further suggested that the steam engine could be used for pushing carriages. This idea made Watt think. He then made a miniature model using tin steam cylinders and pistons attached to it to drive wheels with the help of a system of gears. He had however abandoned his search on steam engines soon after. Now, while examining the Newcomen steam engine, Watt remembered his own experiments and once again his interest in understanding and making better models of steam engine was renewed. This time, with renewed interest, he began researching on the properties of steam.

When he conducted his experiments, at first he used apothecaries' trials and hollow canes for steam reservoirs and pipes. He later used a Papin's digester and also a common syringe. The latter combination he found suitable and made a non condensing engine. In this engine, he used steam at a pressure of 15 pounds per square inch. He worked the valve by hand, and soon he saw that an automatic valve gear was needed to make a working machine. He, however, did not succeed in his experiment. Watt then, first repaired the

Miniature *something small, probably a painting or a portrait*
Piston *is part of a machine moving upwards and downwards in a cylinder to make other parts of the engine move*
Apothecary *a pharmacist or a druggist*
Reservoir *a place where water is collected for later usage*

Newcomen model of the steam engine, though it still did not work properly, and then continued with his experiments. While repairing the model, Watt saw that the boiler of the steam engine was made to scale but even then the boiler was incapable of furnishing enough steam to power the engine.

Problem With the Newcomen Model

Watt realized that about three-quarters of the heat of the steam was wasted as it was used in heating the engine cylinder on every cycle. Also, cold water was injected into the cylinder in order to reduce the pressure of the steam through condensation. The engine therefore wasted the energy in repeatedly keeping the cylinder heated. As a result less mechanical force was being produced. He saw that these were the flaws with the Newcomen model of the steam engine.

James Watt then began conducting experiments to improve the boiler. For his experiments, he constructed a new boiler where he could measure the amount of water evaporated and the steam condensed at each stroke of the engine.

Condensation *it is the process where gas is reduced to a liquid state*

James Watt Rediscovers Latent Heat

While conducting his experiments, Watt discovered that it required a very small amount of steam to heat a large quantity of water. He immediately began determining with precision the relative weights of steam and water in the steam cylinder when the process of condensation took place at the down stroke of the engine. It was then that Watt was able to independently prove the existence of "latent heat", which had already been discovered by scientist, Joseph Black, who was also a friend of Watt. With his new research, Watt went to Black who in turn helped Watt better understand the workings of latent heat. Watt was now certain that at the boiling point, the condensing steam was capable of heating six times its weight of water which was used for the process

Drawing of his steam engine

Latent heat is the heat absorbed or released by a substance to change the solid to a liquid or a gas or vice versa

of condensation and thus the mechanical energy was getting wasted.

Watt Improvises With a Separate Condenser

Watt saw the importance of taking greater care to economize steam than had previously been attempted. At first, he economized in the boiler, and made boilers with wooden "shells" in order to prevent any losses by conduction and radiation, and used a larger number of flues to secure more absorption of the heat from the furnace gases. He also covered his steam pipes with nonconducting materials, and took every precaution to secure the complete utilization of the heat during combustion. He soon discovered that the action of the steam in the cylinder was responsible for the loss of heat.

After his scientific investigations, James Watt worked on improving the steam engine with an intelligent understanding of its existing defects, and with knowledge of its cause. Watt soon saw that in order to reduce the losses in the working of the steam in the steam cylinder, it was necessary to find a way to keep the cylinder always as hot as the steam that entered it.

James Watt Writes

James Watt wrote: "I had gone to take a walk on a fine Sabbath afternoon. I had entered the Green by the gate at the foot of Charlotte street, and had passed the old washing house. I was thinking upon the engine at the time, and had gone as far as the herd's house, when the idea came into my mind that, as steam was an elastic body, it would rush into a vacuum, and, if a communication were made between the cylinder and an exhausted vessel, it would rush into it, and might be there condensed without cooling the cylinder. I then saw that I must get rid of the condensed steam and injection water if I used a jet, as in Newcomen's engine. Two ways of doing this occurred to me: First, the water might be run off by a descending pipe... The second was, to make the pump large enough to extract both water and air. I had not walked farther than the Golf house, when the whole thing was arranged in my mind."

The Solution

Then, in May 1765, Watt thought of a way to produce more mechanical power. The solution to the problem was simply to have a separate chamber apart from the piston to condense the steam while maintaining the temperature of the cylinder at the same temperature as the injected steam. This was done by surrounding the cylinder with a steam jacket. This meant that very little heat was absorbed into the cylinder during each cycle and more heat was generated to perform work. Based on this concept Watt did not long to develop his model of the steam engine.

Model of Watt's steam engine

James Watt had invented his all-important separate condenser. He began constructing a smaller version of his steam engine with a separate condenser. He then proceeded to make an experimental test of his new invention. After a lot of effort and hard work, he managed to make his model. It was a crude model and did not work as efficiently as expected but it did produce more mechanical power. Encouraged by his experiment, Watt started to improve his model.

Soon, he began the construction of a larger model based on his steam engine. Having taken this first step and making such a radical improvement, the success of this invention was followed by more acclaim.

After James Watt had built his larger experimental engine, he hired a room in an old deserted pottery. There he worked with mechanic Folm Gardiner. During this time, Watt met Doctor John Roebuck, a wealthy physician, one of the founders of Carron Iron Works. Now, Watt had a workable design of the steam engine but he lacked finances. Black had been providing Watt with money but it wasn't enough. So, John Roebuck gave the necessary money required to Watt though a large part of it was invested in getting the patent for Watt's invention. Due to lack of funds Watt was forced to work as a civil engineer for eight years.

In 1768, James Watt met Matthew Boulton, while he was heading to London to get his patent. Matthew Boulton wanted to buy an interest in the patent. With Roebuck's consent, Watt offered Matthew Boulton a one third interest. Subsequently, Roebuck proposed to transfer to Matthew Boulton, one half of his proprietorship in Watt's inventions, for a sum of one thousand pounds. Sometime later, when Roebuck became bankrupt, it was Matthew Boulton, who came to help Watt. The partnership between Watt and Boulton was successful and lasted for twenty five years.

First Engines

In 1776, the engines designed by Watt were being installed in many commercial enterprises. They were used to power pumps and produced only reciprocating motion to move the pump rods at

Bankrupt *is a person who is unable to pay his or her debts and is judged so by the court*

the bottom of the shaft. The next five years, Watt continued to install the steam engines. Now that the steam engine was hugely successful, Boulton urged Watt to innovate further so that the steam engine could be used for grinding, weaving and milling.

For the next few years, Watt continued to improve and modify his design of the steam engine. Among the improvements was the use of the steam indicator which told about the pressure of the steam inside the cylinder against its volume. Watt kept this as his trade secret. Another important invention, about which Watt was immensely proud, was the creation of parallel motion required in double-acting engines as it produced the straight line motion required for the cylinder rod and pump, from the connected rocking beam, whose end moved in a circular arc. This improvement was patented in 1784. These improvements made the steam engine designed by Watt five times more fuel efficient than the Newcomen Model.

Later Years

Watt's steam engine was a great success. He, however, did not stop there and continued to invent. Among his other notable inventions was the copying machine. It was in 1780 that he had the patent for the copying machine.

Together, Watt and Boulton started the Soho Manufactory to manufacture their engines. The manufactory opened in 1796. In 1800s Watt retired. By now, Watt's sons, Gregory and James Jr, were managing the enterprise. Even after his retirement, Watt continued to invent in his workshop at his home in Handsworth Heath, Staffordshire. His interest in civil engineering remained and he was often consulted on various projects. He later died on August 25, 1819 at the age of 83.

LOUIS BRAILLE

Louis Braille was merely a boy when he developed a system for educating the blind by touch. The Braille System, named after him, had helped educate all those who are blind over many decades. Born in 1809 in France, Braille became blind by the age of 5. It was through, his intelligence and determination to read that he opened the door of knowledge for all those who could not see.

Early Life and the Fatal Accident

Louis Braille was born in Coupvray, France, on January 4, 1809. He was the fourth and the last child of Simon-René and Monique Braille. He had three elder siblings- Monique Catherine Josephine Braille (b.1793), Louis-Simon Braille (b.1795), and Marie Celine Braille (b.1797). His father had three hectares of land and vineyards. Simon-René also had a successful enterprise as the developer of leather and maker of horse tack.

No sooner had Louis learnt to walk that he began playing in his father's workshop. One day, when Louis was three years old, he was playing with some of his father's tools, trying to make a hole in a piece of leather with an awl. Unconsciously, Louis was squinting too close to the surface and had pressed down hard to drive the point in the leather. Suddenly, the awl pierced the leather with force and at the same time struck the child's eye.

Hearing the agonized scream of the child, his father rushed inside. Immediately, he took the crying child to the local physician who bound and patched the child's eye. He also made arrangements so that

Simon-René could take young Louis to a surgeon in Paris tomorrow. However, no treatment was able to save the child's eye. Over the next few weeks after the accident, the child suffered greatly as the infection in the damaged eye spread to the other eye as well.

The infection Louis was able to bear but by the time he was five years of age, he had lost his sight completely in both the eyes. His parents, however, made all efforts to raise him like a normal child. In their affection and care, Louis never felt that he could not see. With the help of the cane that his father made for him, he learnt to navigate around the village and the paths that surrounded the village.

Education

Louis was a bright and intelligent child. Seeing his enthusiasm and ability, his father decided to put him in a school along with the sighted students. By the age of 10, he had learnt all that he was taught at the local school. Louis was an excellent student with an exceptional memory.

Navigate to make way or to find a way; to direct a ship or an aircraft in a particular direction often by using maps

In 1819, Braille was sent to study in perhaps one of the first school for blind children, *National Institute of Blind Youth* situated in Paris. The school was founded by Valentin Haüy. The school wasn't big but it provided blind children an opportunity to learn together.

Haüy System of Education

At the institute, the blind children were taught through a unique method which was invented by the school's founder, Valentin Haüy. Haüy who was not blind had decided to devote his life helping the blind. He had, therefore, designed and formed a small library of books for the blind children. He did so by using a technique of embossing heavy paper with the raised imprints of Latin letters. So, when the children would trace their fingers over the letters they would be able to read what was written on the paper.

Louis Braille like the other blind children was able to read through this method but the method had a disadvantage. Though the children could read but they were unable to write. This inability to write struck young Braille. It was more so because he

Emboss to put a raised design or writing on a surface; on paper, leather, clothes etc
Imprint a mark which is printed on something; a mark made by pressing

could not write letters back home. Also, he felt that the text they were taught was kept deliberately small.

Meanwhile, the books crafted by Haüy were large and heavy. Though the books were a bit of a bother but they could make the blind read and those with sight could easily understand what was written in them. At that time, as there were lack of schools and books for the blind, the Haüy system was thought to be the best system available for teaching the blind. Also these books provided the best possible result. Braille and his schoolmates, however, could easily see the drawbacks of these books. Nonetheless, Haüy's system had provided a reasonable breakthrough in educating the blind as recognition through the sense of touch proved to be a workable strategy for sightless reading.

Learning to Play Music

Braille read the Haüy books repeatedly and thoroughly. He also paid tremendous attention to the oral instructions given at the school. He excelled in his studies and proved to be a proficient student. No sooner had Braille completed his studies that

Proficient it is the ability to do something skilfully after learning and training

he was asked to stay behind and become a teacher at the school. So, in 1883, Braille had become one of the teachers at the school. He continued to teach history, geometry and algebra at the school to the end of his life.

Braille also had a keen ear for music. So, he also learnt to play organ and the cello. He was so accomplished in playing music that he played organ for churches all over France.

Night Writing

While, Braille was studying at the institute, he heard of a system developed by Captain Charles Barbier in 1821. The system developed by the captain was called "night writing". According to the system, embossed symbols stood out of the surface. The symbols could only be understood by tracing fingers on the symbols. It thus became a coded method for the soldiers to send information silently at night on the battlefield.

As luck would have it, Captain Charles Barbier visited the institute and Braille was inspired by the lecture that the captain gave about the "night writing". His system was coded and consisted of dots and dashes that were impressed on thick paper. Though Braille thought that the system of the captain was a bit complex but nonetheless it inspired him to form his own system of reading and writing for the blind. The system that he developed replaced the embossed books available at the institute.

Developing the Braille System

Braille was determined to develop a system of reading and writing that would help decrease the gap between the blind and the sighted. Inspired by the system developed by Captain Barbier, Braille had developed his own system in 1824. He was merely 15 years of age. Braille had developed his own system by simplifying the form though increasing the efficiency of the system of "night writing". His system was based on the twenty-six letters of the alphabet. Braille reduced the number of dots from twelve to six and placed the letters in a uniform order for better recognition. He published his system in 1829. Later, by 1837, he even removed the dashes that were used by the captain as they were difficult to understand. Like the captain's system, fingers needed to be traced over the symbols to understand and read them.

a	b	c	d	e	f	g	h	i	j
1	12	14	145	15	124	1245	125	24	245

k	l	m	n	o	p	q	r	s	t
13	123	134	1345	135	1234	12345	1235	234	2345

u	v	w	x	y	z
136	1236	2456	1346	13456	1356

The Braille Cell

1 ● ● 4
2 ● ● 5
3 ● ● 6

The Braille alphabet

By changing the number and placement of dots, Braille coded letters, punctuation, numbers, familiar words, scientific symbols, mathematical and musical notation, and capitalization. This method proved to be immensely useful as the readers understood and grasped the letter quickly. Using the Braille system, enabled the students to take notes and even write by punching dots into the paper with a pointed instrument.

Notation *it is a system where certain specified symbols are used to represent words*

King Louis Philippe was greatly impressed by the Braille system after he had seen the public demonstration of the system at the Paris Exposition of Industry in 1834. Braille's fellow students meanwhile loved this new system. In no time this system was so popular that sighted instructors and school boards grew worried that soon the educated blind individuals would take away their jobs. They thus remained stuck with Haüy's embossed-letter system.

Later Life

In 1839, Braille published details of a method he had developed for communication with sighted people, using patterns of dots to approximate the shape of printed symbols. He even helped his friend Pierre Foucault in developing a device that could emboss letters like a typewriter. Foucault's machine became a great success during the 1855 World's Fair in Paris.

Though Braille was admired and respected by his pupils, his writing system could not become part of the institute curriculum until after his death.

Curriculum the subjects forming part of the course taught in a school or college

The successors of Valentin Haüy, did not show any interest in adopting the Braille system. Dr. Alexandre François-René Pignier, headmaster at the school, was dismissed when he had a history book translated into braille.

Meanwhile, after an ailing health which worsened with age due to a lung infection, Braille left his job as a teacher in 1840. When his condition worsened still, he was taken back to his family home in Coupvray. He died at his home in 1852, two days after he had turned forty-three.

Recognition After Death

Shortly before Braille's death, a former student of Braille who was a blind musician, performed in Paris, France. During his performance she let the audience know that all that she had learnt was through the Braille system developed for the blind. This created renewed interest in and a revival of the Braille system. However, the system as only fully adopted in 1854, two years after Louis Braille's death. The system, however, is still is use though with some modifications from time to time.

Revival bringing something back in use or making something popular again